Travel guide to Chennai 2024

Chennai: Where Tradition Meets Modernity - Your Ultimate Travel Guide

Luna Arlet

All Right Reserved!

No Part of this book may be reproduced, stored in a retrieval system, or transmitted in any form or by any means, electronic or mechanical, photocopying, recording or otherwise, without the prior written permission of the copyright owner

Copyright © Luna Arlet, 2024

Table of contents
- **WELCOME TO CHENNAI**
- **HOW TO GET THERE**
- **TRANSPORTATION IN CHENNAI**
- **SIGHTSEEING IN CHENNAI**
- **BUDGET SHOPPING IN CHENNAI**
- **CHENNAI'S CUISINE**
- **LAKES AND GARDENS**
- **NIGHTLIFE AND ENTERTAINMENT**
- **DAY TRIPS FROM CHENNAI**
- **PRACTICAL TIPS**
- **USEFUL PHRASES AND LANGUAGE TIPS**
- **RECAP**

WELCOME TO CHENNAI

Often referred to as the "Gateway to South India," Chennai is a thriving city on India's southeast coast. Chennai, the capital city of Tamil Nadu, was formerly known as Madras.

It is a major centre for education, business, and culture in the area. Chennai provides tourists with an exceptional fusion of tradition and modernity because of its rich history, dynamic culture, and diversified population.

Overview

Chennai, with a total area of over 426 square kilometres, is the fourth-largest metropolis in India. It is renowned for its lively ambiance, busy streets, and thriving business sector.

The city's cosmopolitan nature is influenced by the melting pot of cultures that draws visitors from all over the nation and the globe.

Chennai has traditionally been an important port city and a hub for trade and commerce thanks to its advantageous location along the Bay of Bengal.

It is still a major economic centre today, with booming companies in fields including banking, information technology, healthcare, and auto manufacturing.

<u>Prehistory</u>

Madraspatnam, a fishing village, was the name given to Chennai when it was first settled more than 2,000 years ago. Later, a number of kingdoms, including the Pallavas, Cholas, and Vijayanagara Empire, ruled over the area.

British influence began in the region when the British East India Company built

Fort St. George, a fortified settlement, in the 17th century.

Madras became the capital of the Madras Presidency and a major trading hub during the British colonial era. The city developed into a significant military and administrative hub and played a critical role in colonial governance.

Its current identity was shaped by major advancements in governance, infrastructure, and education over time.

The name Chennai was formally changed by the government in 1996 to reflect the nearby village of Chennapattanam. The goal of this modification was to showcase the city's Tamil heritage and advance its cultural identity internationally.

Language and Culture

Chennai is proud of its rich cultural legacy, which is firmly ingrained in Tamil customs and traditions. The city is well-known for its centuries-old classical dance, literature, music, and art forms.

Chennai's cultural environment is largely shaped by classical Carnatic music and Bharatanatyam dance, which are taught at a multitude of institutions and academies committed to their promotion and preservation.

Chennai's predominant language is Tamil, which reflects the region's predominately Tamilian population. However the city's global character also attracts residents from a variety of language and cultural backgrounds, adding to its linguistic diversity.

Chennai's culinary scene offers a delicious selection of South Indian foods, including dosas, idlis, sambar, and seafood specialties, further reflecting the city's cultural diversity.

The street food scene in the city is especially lively, with roadside vendors and busy marketplaces offering delectable snacks and sweets.

In conclusion, Chennai is a bustling city with a varied population, a lively culture, and a rich past. Chennai is a fascinating place to explore, drawing visitors with its unique blend of tradition and innovation from its ancient roots to its current advances.

HOW TO GET THERE

On India's southeast coast, the vibrant metropolis of Chennai serves as the capital of Tamil Nadu. Chennai draws tourists from all over the world because of its thriving economy, dynamic atmosphere, and rich cultural legacy.

Chennai's well-connected transportation system makes getting there, whether travelling domestically or abroad, rather easy.

Through Air

The third-busiest airport in India in terms of passenger traffic, Chennai International Airport serves the city. Situated in the Meenambakkam area, roughly 21 kilometres to the southwest of the city centre, the airport serves both domestic and international travel, with multiple airlines operating out of it.

Domestic passengers can easily fly from major Indian cities including Delhi, Mumbai, Kolkata, Bengaluru, and Hyderabad to Chennai.

Many airlines offer regular flights to Chennai, giving travellers a variety of alternatives. These airlines include Air India, IndiGo, SpiceJet, and GoAir.

Chennai International Airport connects the city to locations throughout Asia, Europe, the Middle East, and beyond, providing direct flights that act as a gateway to South India for visitors from outside the region.

Travellers from overseas can easily connect to Chennai because of the regular international flights offered by airlines like Emirates, Singapore Airlines, British Airways, and Qatar Airways.

Passengers may easily reach their final destination within the city after landing at Chennai International Airport thanks to the variety of ground transportation choices available, such as pre-paid taxis, app-based ride-hailing services, and airport shuttles.

Via Train

One of the biggest railway networks in the world, Indian Railways, runs a vast train network that connects Chennai to the rest of India. The city's two primary train stations, Chennai Central and Chennai Egmore, act as important hubs for long-distance and suburban train services.

Trains from northern and western regions of India, including places like Delhi, Mumbai, Kolkata, and Hyderabad, are handled by Chennai Central, which is situated in Park Town.

Chennai Egmore is an Egmore station that mostly handles trains from the south and east. These trains connect Chennai to places like Bengaluru, Coimbatore, Madurai, and Tiruchirappalli.

There are numerous notable trains that run to and from Chennai, providing travellers with convenient and effective rail travel options. These trains include the Rajdhani Express, Shatabdi Express, and Duronto Express.

Furthermore, suburban trains offer reasonably priced and practical modes of transportation for commuters moving throughout the Chennai metropolitan area and its surrounding areas.

Train travel to Chennai is a popular option for both domestic and foreign tourists since it allows travellers to take in picturesque rural vistas, discover the rich cultural diversity of India, and fully experience the allure of train travel.

<u>By Route</u>

A large network of state highways, national highways, and arterial roads connects Chennai to other cities and states. The city is well connected by road to locations both inside and outside of Tamil Nadu, making it a key hub for transportation in South India.

The two primary highways that link Chennai to other important cities and states are National Highway 48 (NH48) and National Highway 32 (NH32).

While NH32 connects Chennai to Tirupati in Andhra Pradesh, NH48 links the city to Bengaluru in Karnataka. State highways and arterial roads also facilitate easy road travel by connecting neighbouring towns and districts.

By road, getting to Chennai gives you the freedom to explore picturesque routes, stop at noteworthy locations, and take in South India's varied landscapes. Whether travelling to Chennai by road in a private automobile, bus, or cab, visitors can have a convenient and enjoyable trip.

In conclusion, Chennai's sophisticated transportation system makes travelling there easy and accessible. Visitors to Chennai may anticipate a smooth journey and a warm welcome to the energetic and culturally diverse city on India's southeast coast, regardless of how they choose to get there—by plane, rail, or automobile.

ACCOMODATION

Chennai, the energetic capital of Tamil Nadu, has a wide variety of lodging choices to meet the demands of all types of tourists, from luxury travellers to backpackers on a tight budget.

Chennai offers lodging options to fit every taste and budget, whether you're searching for luxurious hotels, quaint guesthouses, or reasonably priced low-cost lodging.

Resorts

Chennai is home to a large number of boutique hotels, business hotels, and luxury hotels that provide upscale amenities and first-rate service to discerning tourists.

Hotels in Chennai offer opulent lodging, exquisite dining options, and cutting-edge amenities to suit the needs of both business and leisure tourists. These accommodations range from independent enterprises to five-star chains.

Luxurious hotels in Chennai, such as the Taj Coromandel, The Leela Palace, and ITC Grand Chola, are the pinnacles of luxury and extravagance; they include large rooms, fine dining options, spa treatments, and attentive service.

Corporate travellers are catered to by business hotels such as the Hilton Chennai, Hyatt Regency, and Radisson Blu, which offer state-of-the-art conference rooms, executive suites, and business centres.

Chennai provides a range of quaint boutique hotels and heritage properties, like The Park Chennai, Somerset Greenways, and The Raintree Hotel, for those looking for a more personal and boutique experience.

These establishments offer visitors a distinctive and unforgettable experience by fusing modern architecture with regional charm.

Guesthouses

For those looking for a quaint and private setting, guesthouses and bed-and-breakfasts provide a more customised and comfortable stay.

All of Chennai's guesthouses, from boutique properties to family-run businesses, provide friendly service, cosy lodgings, and an insight into the local way of life.

Located in residential areas like Mylapore, Alwarpet, and Nungambakkam, guesthouses provide visitors with a peaceful haven from the bustle of the city.

Large rooms, verdant gardens, and home-cooked meals made with products that are found locally are common features of these houses, which provide visitors with a warm and laid-back atmosphere.

Popular guesthouses in Chennai that provide a distinctive fusion of comfort, convenience, and individualised service are Raj Palace Sundar, Belstead Bungalow, and Hanu Reddy Residences.

Whether you're on a romantic break, travelling with family, or travelling alone, guesthouses offer a reasonably priced and appealing substitute for standard hotels.

Still Within Budget

Chennai provides a large selection of inexpensive hotels, hostels, and backpacker accommodations for tourists on a tight budget; these options are reasonably priced without sacrificing convenience or comfort.

These low-cost lodging options provide tidy and pleasant lodging at prices that are affordable for families, lone travellers, and backpackers.

In Chennai, low-cost lodging options including Hotel Pearl International, Hotel Peninsula, and Hotel Mars offer standard features like free Wi-Fi, tidy rooms, and attached bathrooms, guaranteeing a comfortable stay at a reasonable cost.

Budget hotels are perfect for tourists on a low budget because many of them are conveniently positioned close to popular tourist destinations, dining establishments, and transit hubs.

Budget travellers also like hostels and backpackers because they provide shared facilities, dormitory-style lodging, and the chance to meet other tourists from around the globe.

For those on a single trip or a backpacker seeking companionship, hostels such as Zostel Chennai, Red Lollipop Hostel, and Backpacker Panda Chennai provide reasonably priced lodging in a community setting.

To sum up, there are a variety of lodging alternatives available in Chennai to suit a wide range of tastes and price points, so any visitor can find the ideal spot to stay while visiting this energetic city.

Chennai has lodging options to fit every taste and budget, whether you're more interested in the opulence of a five-star hotel, the charm of a boutique guesthouse, or the affordability of a low-cost stay.

TRANSPORTATION IN CHENNAI

To meet the demands of both locals and visitors, Chennai, a thriving metropolis on India's southeast coast, provides a range of transportation alternatives.

Navigating Chennai is rather easy and convenient, with its effective public transportation networks, convenient taxi services, and affordable car rentals.

Public Transportation

Chennai has a well-established public transportation system that includes suburban trains and buses run by Indian Railways and the Chennai Metropolitan Transport Corporation (CMTC), respectively.

In Chennai, buses are the main form of public transportation. A sizable fleet of buses, run by the government and the private sector, covers routes all across the city and its outskirts.

The CMTC runs an extensive bus route network that links important residential neighbourhoods, business centres, and tourism destinations. Buses are an economical and practical way to get to

Chennai, with frequent services and reasonable costs.

Suburban trains, in addition to buses, offer a productive way to go around Chennai and its surrounding cities and districts. Major train stations, Chennai Central and Chennai Egmore, provide suburban train services to a number of locations throughout the Chennai metropolitan area.

Because they provide a dependable and timely means of transportation, commuters going to and from the city's suburbs, especially like these trains.

Autorickshaws and Taxis

In Chennai, taxis and auto rickshaws are well-liked means of transportation for both residents and visitors, providing an easy method to get from place to place both inside the city and outside of it.

Metered taxis, run by several taxi firms, are widely accessible in Chennai and provide passengers with on-demand transportation options. You can use smartphone apps to reserve these cabs, call them on the street, or make reservations through hotel concierge services.

When looking for a dependable and comfortable private transportation alternative with fixed fares, metered taxis offer a comfortable and convenient choice.

Auto rickshaws, commonly referred to as "autos" or "tuk-tuks," are a common sight on Chennai's streets, offering a reasonably priced and effective way to get around for short distances.

Larger cars may find it difficult to manoeuvre through crowded neighbourhoods and tiny alleys, which is why auto rickshaws are so popular.

Although passengers usually bargain with the driver for a rate based on the distance covered, they can book auto rickshaws and guarantee reasonable prices by using ride-hailing applications.

Cars for Rent

Renting a car is a terrific way for those who want more freedom and flexibility to explore Chennai and the surrounding areas at their own leisure.

In Chennai, there are numerous car rental businesses that provide both short- and long-term rentals of a variety of vehicles, including sedans, SUVs, and luxury cars.

Travellers can experience the flexibility of self-guided exploration, visit off-the-beaten-path locations, and tailor their itinerary by renting a car.

In addition, two-wheeler rentals are well-liked by both visitors and residents since they provide a practical and affordable means of navigating Chennai's crowded streets. Renting a scooter or a motorcycle from a variety of rental companies gives tourists the freedom and agility to explore cities.

In conclusion, Chennai's transportation system provides a range of choices to accommodate visitors' tastes and financial constraints.

Whether travelling by public transportation, renting a car, or using taxis and auto-rickshaws, getting around

Chennai is easy and convenient, making it possible for visitors to easily see the energetic city and its environs.

SIGHTSEEING IN CHENNAI

Discover the wealth of historical sites, architectural wonders, and natural attractions in Chennai, the cultural centre of South India.

Chennai has a wealth of things to view that highlight its colourful culture and rich history, from stunning beaches to historic temples and colonial forts.

Seaside

One of the world's longest urban beaches, Marina Beach is a well-liked tourist and local attraction that stretches along Chennai's eastern shore. Marina Beach is a charming location for strolls, picnics, and water sports due to its golden sands, mild waves, and breathtaking sunsets.

A must-visit location for anybody visiting Chennai, visitors may also take in sights like the famous lighthouse, the Anna Memorial, and the busy Marina Promenade.

Temple of Kapaleeshwarar

Lord Shiva is the focus of the ancient Hindu temple known as Kapaleeshwarar

Temple, which is situated in the busy Mylapore district.

This stunning temple, which dates to the 7th century, is well-known for its Dravidian architecture, elaborately carved gopurams (towering entrances), and colourful statues that represent Hindu mythology.

The temple is a spiritual and cultural icon in Chennai where guests can observe daily rituals, participate in religious events, and be in awe of its architectural magnificence.

Georgetown, Fort

The administrative centre of the Tamil Nadu government is located in Fort St. George, a historic fortress constructed in the 17th century by the British East India Company.

Situated in the centre of Chennai, this well-preserved fort is home to a number of important buildings, such as the oldest Anglican church in India, St. Mary's Church, and the Fort Museum, which features colonial-era antiques, paintings, and souvenirs.

Discover more about Chennai's British and colonial past by exploring the fort's walls, cannons, and colonial architecture.

Government Museum

One of the biggest and oldest museums in India, the Government Museum was founded in 1851 and features an extensive collection of artwork, antiques, and archeological finds.

This expansive museum, which is situated in the Egmore district, features galleries devoted to anthropology, art, natural history, numismatics, and archaeology.

These galleries provide visitors with an insight into India's rich cultural legacy and historical civilizations. History lovers and art lovers should not miss the Bronze Gallery, the Amaravati Gallery, and the Museum Theatre, among other highlights.

Basilica of Santhome Cathedral

Situated in the Santhome area, the Santhome Cathedral Basilica is a highly esteemed Catholic pilgrimage site devoted to St. Thomas the Apostle.

This magnificent church, which was constructed on the location where it is thought that St. Thomas was buried, has neo-Gothic architecture, stained glass windows, and elaborate altars that give guests a calm and spiritual atmosphere.

In addition, the cathedral has artefacts and relics related to St. Thomas, drawing pilgrims from all over the world who are looking for spiritual comfort and benefits.

In conclusion, visitors wishing to experience Chennai's rich history, dynamic culture, and breathtaking natural surroundings will find a multitude of tourist options available to them.

Discovering the city's colonial past at Fort St. George, admiring the architecture of Kapaleeshwarar Temple, or basking in the sun at Marina Beach—Centra's landmarks and attractions ensure that tourists of all ages and interests have an amazing time.

BUDGET SHOPPING IN CHENNAI

Chennai, a thriving city on India's southeast coast, has a thriving retail environment that appeals to both locals and visitors' wide range of interests and preferences.

With its vibrant marketplaces and bazaars as well as its contemporary malls and shopping centres, Chennai offers countless chances to indulge in retail therapy and find one-of-a-kind finds to bring home.

Bazaars and Markets

Chennai is well known for its bustling marketplaces and bazaars, where both locals and tourists congregate to purchase a wide range of products, including fresh vegetables, spices, and traditional fabrics and handicrafts.

The GeorgeTown neighbourhood, which is home to the busy Parry's Corner and the storied Moore Market, is home to one of Chennai's most recognizable markets.

Discover a maze of little streets brimming with stores offering a wide range of merchandise, from electronics and home goods to apparel and accessories. T. Nagar, Purasawalkam, and Ranganathan Street are a few other well-liked markets in Chennai that provide a distinctive shopping experience and a window into the vibrant street life of the city.

Retail Stores and Malls

Chennai has a wide variety of malls and shopping centres that suit every taste and budget for those looking for a more contemporary and practical shopping experience.

One of Chennai's top shopping locations, Express Avenue is situated in the centre of the business district and offers a variety of local and international brands, high-end boutiques, and entertainment options like food courts and movie theatres.

Another well-liked mall is Phoenix MarketCity, which is situated in Velachery. It is well-known for its wide selection of retail stores, restaurants, and entertainment venues, making it a one-stop location for dining, shopping, and leisure activities.

Ampa Skywalk, Spencer Plaza, and Forum Vijaya Mall are a few other well-known malls in Chennai that provide a wide range of shops and services to suit the needs of customers of all ages and interests.

Artisans and Memorabilia

In addition, Chennai is a veritable gold mine of handicrafts and memorabilia that provide tourists with the chance to bring distinctive keepsakes of their trip to the city home.

Travellers wishing to fully experience Chennai's rich cultural legacy are drawn to handcrafted items like bronze sculptures, Tanjore paintings, and traditional Kanchipuram silk sarees.

These handcrafted gems can be purchased by tourists at government-run emporiums like Poompuhar Handicrafts Emporium and Tamil Nadu Handicrafts

Development Corporation, as well as specialty stores and boutiques in localities like Mylapore, T. Nagar, and Kotturpuram.

Furthermore, street sellers and markets frequently provide a range of handcrafted items, jewellery, and trinkets at reasonable costs, enabling tourists to purchase mementos while taking in Chennai's lively street culture.

In conclusion, whether you're looking for exclusive handicrafts and souvenirs, exploring vibrant marketplaces and bazaars, or indulging in retail therapy at contemporary malls, shopping in Chennai is a fascinating experience that has something to offer everyone.

Chennai delivers a remarkable shopping experience that captures the essence of the city's dynamic character and rich cultural legacy. This is made possible by its wide variety of shopping venues and lively retail environment.

CHENNAI'S CUISINE

The diversified cultural background and culinary traditions of Chennai, the gastronomic capital of South India, are reflected in its rich tapestry of flavours and fragrances.

Chennai's culinary culture is a melting pot of flavours, textures, and spices that entice the taste buds of locals and visitors alike, offering everything from traditional

South Indian delicacies to worldwide fusion food.

Regional Specialties

The traditional South Indian cuisine of Chennai is well-known for its rice-based meals, aromatic curries, and a variety of chutneys and accompaniments. The dosa, a thin, crispy pancake cooked from fermented rice and lentil batter and served with a variety of savoury toppings including potato masala, paneer, and spicy chutneys, is one of Chennai's most famous dishes.

Sambar, a zesty lentil stew, and coconut chutney are served alongside the soft and fluffy steamed rice cakes known as idli, which is another favourite.

The distinctive flavours and ingredients of South Indian cuisine are showcased in vada (deep-fried lentil fritters), Pongal (savoury rice and lentil porridge), and biryani (fragrant rice dish cooked with meat or vegetables and aromatic spices).

Well-liked Eateries

Chennai is home to a wide variety of eateries, cafes, and restaurants with cuisines ranging from foreign to traditional South Indian, to suit every taste and preference.

Visit well-known restaurants like Saravana Bhavan, Murugan Idli Shop, and Adyar Ananda Bhavan, which are renowned for their mouthwatering dosas, idlis, and vadas served in a laid-back atmosphere, for a genuine flavour of Chennai's culinary heritage.

For those who are in the mood for something exotic, try fine dining establishments such as Dakshin at the ITC Grand Chola, which provides a gourmet dining experience with South Indian specialties prepared in a contemporary way, or Annalakshmi, a vegetarian restaurant renowned for its large buffet spread of Indian and international dishes served in a calm and giving atmosphere.

Food on the Street

With a mouthwatering selection of tasty, reasonably priced, and incredibly filling street food options, Chennai's busy streets are a food lover's dream come true.

Chennai's street food scene is a sensory extravaganza that tantalises the senses and awakens the palate, offering everything from spicy spices to savoury munchies.

Street food vendors along Marina Beach and other popular spots serve delicious street food such as sundal, which is a nutritious snack made from boiled chickpeas or lentils seasoned with coconut, mustard seeds, and curry leaves.

Other must-try street food delicacies include bajji, which are deep-fried fritters made from assorted vegetables like chili peppers, onions, and potatoes, served with tangy chutneys.

In summary, Chennai's food is a dynamic tapestry of tastes, textures, and scents that captures the city's diverse cultural background and rich culinary history.

Chennai provides a gastronomic journey that satisfies the senses and makes an enduring impression on tourists from all over the world, whether they are indulging in flavorful street food delights, sampling traditional South Indian delicacies at renowned restaurants, or discovering global fusion cuisine at upscale eateries.

LAKES AND GARDENS

Lakes and gardens are peaceful oases amidst Chennai's busy metropolitan landscape, offering visitors and locals alike a break from the bustle of daily life.

These natural areas are essential to the city's cultural fabric because they provide chances for leisure, relaxation, and connection with the natural world

Lakes

There are many beautiful lakes in Chennai, each with its own distinct charm and personality. The largest and most recognizable of them is the vast urban lake that runs the whole length of the city's eastern shore, called Chennai Marina.

Situated along the blue seas of the Bay of Bengal, Marina Beach is a well-liked spot for strolls, picnics, and beachfront pursuits. Along Marina Lake, visitors can also take pleasure in boat rides and sunset views, finding moments of peace despite the busy cityscape

Situated in the centre of Chennai, amidst abundant greenery, is the tranquil Chetpet Lake, which is another noteworthy lake.

With its magnificent overlooks, boating facilities, and running pathways, this man-made lake offers a tranquil haven from the bustle of the city. It is a welcome break for both fitness fanatics and nature lover

Gardens

With its many beautifully designed parks and gardens, Chennai offers visitors a chance to get away from the concrete jungle and experience a lush environment.

Situated in the city centre, the Semmozhi Poonga is a botanical garden showcasing a wide range of native and foreign plant species. Explore themed gardens, peaceful ponds, and meandering paths to find a biodiversity oasis right in the middle of Chennai

Another green haven in Chennai is the Huddleston Gardens of the Theosophical Society, which is situated on expansive acres of ground beside the Adyar River.

With its old banyan trees, placid lakes, and verdant lawns, this historic garden offers a tranquil setting for yoga, meditation, and leisurely strolls amid the beauty of nature

Result

In conclusion, Chennai's lakes and parks are essential for improving the city's quality of life since they provide comfort, renewal, and a link to nature amidst the city.

In the middle of the busy bustle of Chennai, tourists can discover moments of quiet and introspection, whether they are taking in the breathtaking views of Marina Beach, the serene atmosphere of Chetpet Lake, or the floral wonders of Semmozhi Poonga.

Lakes and gardens are beloved natural havens that serve as poignant reminders of the value of protecting and fostering green spaces in urban settings so that coming generations can still find inspiration and comfort in the middle of busy city life.

NIGHTLIFE AND ENTERTAINMENT

Chennai, a city renowned for its dynamic energy and thriving cultural scene, provides both residents and visitors with a wide range of entertainment choices and nightlife attractions.

For those looking for fun, relaxation, and cultural immersion, Chennai's entertainment and nightlife scene offers remarkable experiences, ranging from crowded theatres and movies to vibrant nightclubs and bars.

Movies and Theatres

With a booming film industry that produces a wide range of movies in many languages, including Tamil, Telugu, and Hindi, Chennai is a mecca for movie buffs.

The city is home to a large number of theatres and multiplexes that show the newest blockbusters, indie films, and local favourites, giving moviegoers an immersive and enjoyable cinematic experience.

Famous movie theatres like Sathyam Cinemas, Devi Cineplex, and PVR Velachery are well-known for their cutting-edge amenities, cosy seating, and wide range of film options, which make them well-liked hangouts for movie buffs of all ages.

Bars & Nightclubs

With a lively selection of nightclubs, pubs, and lounges that welcome partygoers and music enthusiasts eager to dance the night away, Chennai's nightlife culture really comes to life after dark.

Chennai has an extensive selection of entertainment establishments to suit every taste and desire, ranging from stylish rooftop pubs with breathtaking views of the city to vibrant nightclubs with live DJs and themed parties.

Popular places to go out for drinks at night include Gatsby 2000, Blend - The High Energy Bar, and 10 Downing Street.

Each has a distinct vibe, special cocktails, and lively music that keeps the party going into the wee hours of the morning.

<u>Cultural Exhibitions</u>

Classical music, dance, theatre, and folk performances are just a few of the traditional and modern performing arts that are used to showcase Chennai's rich cultural legacy.

Numerous cultural venues and auditoriums in the city are home to frequent performances by well-known performers and troupes that highlight the rich customs of South Indian culture.

Dance fans can see captivating Bharatanatyam and Kuchipudi performances at locations like Kalakshetra and Bharatiya Vidya Bhavan, while music lovers can enjoy classical Carnatic music concerts at renowned venues like Music Academy and Narada Gana Sabha.

In addition, the dynamic theatre scene in Chennai presents audiences with a wide range of cultural experiences that mirror the artistic vitality and creative spirit of the city through thought-provoking plays, comedies, and experimental performances at locations like Alliance Française, Spaces - The Centre, and Museum Theatre.

To sum up, Chennai's nightlife and entertainment scene provides a wide range of experiences to suit a variety of tastes and interests.

Chennai offers incredible entertainment experiences that highlight the vibrant energy and cultural diversity of the city, whether you're seeing the newest blockbuster at a cutting-edge theatre, dancing the night away at a throbbing nightclub, or immersing yourself in the rich traditions of South Indian culture through music, dance, and theatre.

DAY TRIPS FROM CHENNAI

Located on India's southeast coast, Chennai provides a great starting point for discovering the rich cultural and historical legacy of Tamil Nadu and the surrounding regions.

Chennai provides a plethora of day trip destinations that promise amazing experiences for travellers looking to explore deeper into the region's fascinating history and culture, from tranquil beaches and French colonial villages to ancient temples and UNESCO World Heritage sites.

Pragalipuram

Mahabalipuram, a UNESCO World Heritage site famous for its ancient rock-cut temples, gigantic sculptures, and beautifully carved cave temples, is situated about 55 kilometres south of Chennai.

Known by another name, Mamallapuram, this ancient town attracts tourists from all over the world with its prominent sites including the Shore Temple, Five Rathas, and Arjuna's Penance. Its rich cultural legacy dates back to the Pallava dynasty of the seventh century.

The UNESCO-listed monuments in Mahabalipuram are a great place for day-trippers to explore, and the gorgeous shoreline and local seafood specialties at seaside shacks make it an ideal destination for a cultural and historical excursion from Chennai.

Surroundings

Located around 160 kilometres south of Chennai, Pondicherry, or Puducherry, is a quaint seaside town well-known for its peaceful beaches, spiritual legacy, and French colonial architecture.

Entired with tree-lined boulevards, vibrant colonial buildings, and charming cafes reflecting an old-world elegance reminiscent of its colonial past, Pondicherry provides a unique blend of French and Indian elements.

Pondicherry is a perfect place for a cultural and culinary escape from Chennai, offering day trippers the chance to explore attractions like the French Quarter, Auroville, and the Aurobindo Ashram, unwind on the immaculate beaches of Promenade and Paradise, and indulge in delicious French cuisine at neighbourhood bistros and bakeries.

Puri

Kanchipuram, a historic temple town famous for its magnificent silk sarees, ancient temples, and rich religious heritage, is situated about 75 kilometres southwest of Chennai.

Known as the "City of Thousand Temples," Kanchipuram is home to numerous architectural gems from the Pallava and Chola dynasties. Notable sites like the Varadharaja Perumal Temple, Ekambareswarar Temple, and Kailasanathar Temple highlight the region's rich religious and cultural legacy.

Discover the historic temples, take in the traditional silk weaving demonstrations, and savour delectable South Indian food at neighbourhood restaurants as day visitors experience Kanchipuram's ageless appeal and meditative atmosphere.

To sum up, Chennai is a starting point for a wide range of day trip locations that provide an insight into the natural beauty and rich cultural legacy of Tamil Nadu and the surrounding states.

Whether taking in the French colonial charm of Pondicherry, exploring the ancient rock-cut temples of

Mahabalipuram, or learning about the spiritual treasures of Kanchipuram, day trippers from Chennai are offered a wide range of experiences that are sure to enhance their trip and leave them with enduring memories of South India's cultural and historical splendour.

PRACTICAL TIPS

The dynamic capital of Tamil Nadu, Chennai, provides travellers with an abundance of historical, cultural, and gastronomic activities.

In order to get the most out of your vacation to Chennai, you should be well-prepared with information about local customs, weather patterns, and the ideal time to visit.

Climate and Ideal Time to Go

Chennai has a tropical climate, meaning that it is hot and muggy most of the time. There are three distinct seasons in the city: summer, monsoon, and winter.

Spring (April through June)

Chennai experiences intensely hot summers, frequently reaching highs of above 40 degrees Celsius (104 degrees Fahrenheit). It is advisable to avoid outdoor activities during this season due to the severe and harsh heat.

Monsoon Season (July-September)

The summer heat is relieved during the monsoon season by regular rainfall and lower temperatures. Rain can ruin plans to be outside, but it also infuses the city with lush foliage and a revitalising vibe.

Fall (November through February)

With its moderate temperatures and low humidity, winter is the most pleasant season to visit Chennai. The weather is perfect for taking part in cultural festivals and events, seeing outdoor sites, and relaxing on the beach.

The winter months of October through February are the ideal times to visit Chennai because of the pleasant weather that makes outdoor activities enjoyable.

Guides for Safety

Though traveller safety in Chennai is typically good, it's still important to take some preventative measures to guarantee a hassle-free and easy trip:

Keep Yourself Hydrated: Dehydration can result from Chennai's hot and muggy weather, particularly in the summer. Make sure you stay out of the sun for as long as possible and drink lots of water.

Observe Your Property

Pickpocketing and theft are two common minor crimes in Chennai, much as in any other big city. Avoid carrying big sums of cash, keep your valuables safe, and use caution when visiting busy places and tourist destinations.

Make Use of Dependable Transportation

Choose safe modes of transportation like public transportation, app-based ride-hailing services, and licensed taxis when you're in Chennai. Steer clear of unauthorised taxis and make sure metered charges are applied for transparency's sake.

Observe Local Traditions

Chennai is a historic city with rigid cultural norms. When visiting places of worship, dress modestly, observe local customs and traditions, and avoid making public shows of affection.

Local Protocol

Visitors should be aware of the following particular customs and etiquette that are exclusive to Chennai:

Salutations

In Chennai, it's common to say "Vanakkam" (hello) or "Namaste" (hello/goodbye) when extending a greeting to someone. In official contexts, handshakes are also appropriate; nevertheless, avoid making physical contact with people of the other sex in public.

Coat Code

Given Chennai's conservative culture, modest clothing is advised, particularly when visiting places of worship and cultural events. In public areas, stay away from wearing anything too revealing, such as shorts, tank tops, or sleeveless tops.

Reception of Food

In Chennai, it's common practice to wash your hands both before and after meals. Food is typically served on banana leaves in traditional eateries, and eating with your hands is the norm, while utensils are available for those who would prefer them.

Travellers can have a safe, comfortable, and culturally enlightening trip in Chennai by adhering to these helpful suggestions and showing respect for local customs and etiquette.

This will allow them to fully immerse themselves in the bright energy and rich heritage of this dynamic city.

USEFUL PHRASES AND LANGUAGE TIPS

Travellers get the chance to fully experience South Indian hospitality, food, and culture by visiting Chennai, the energetic capital city of Tamil Nadu.

Even though Tamil is the native tongue of Chennai, knowing a few helpful words in the language might improve your trip and foster a closer relationship with the residents. The following are some crucial expressions and language advice to remember

Simple Expressions

1. Hello: "Vanakkam" (vuh-nuh-kum) is a widely used greeting in Tamil Nadu that is used all day long.

2. Thank you: "Nandri" (nun-dree) - Say "thank you" when someone helps you or shows you hospitality.

3. Yes: "Aama" (ah-mah) - In informal discussions, use this affirmative response.

4. No: "Illai" (ill-eye) - Use this term to express a refusal or a negative reaction.

5. Please: The polite request "Tanga mudiyala" (tang-uh moo-dee-ya-lah) should be made.

6. Pardon me- Say "Kshama panippa" (kshuh-muh puh-nip-pah) to gently draw attention to yourself.

Directions and Navigation

1. Where is...?: "...Enga irukku?" Say "en-gah ee-roo-koo" to request directions to a certain place.

2. Left: "Idam" (ee-dum) - You can use this word to point in the left direction.

3. Right: "Valam" (vah-lum) - This word is used to denote the right direction.
The phrase "Theriyala" (theh-ree-ya-lah) is used to denote travelling straight forward in step four.

Dining and Food

1. Water: In a cafe or restaurant, ask for water by using the term "Thanni" (tun-nee).

2. Vegetarian: Say "Suya virundhu" (soo-yah veer-un-doo) to express your preference for vegetarian cuisine.

3. Spicy: "Pulippu" (poo-lip-poo) – Use this term to express your tolerance for hot and spicy cuisine.

4. Bill, please: Say "Bill, kodunga" (bill koh-dun-guh) to ask for the bill when your dinner is about to end.

Bargaining and Shopping

1. Amount?: "Eppadi?" (ep-pah-dee) – Ask about an item's pricing with this phrase.

2. Expensive: "Mahal" (mah-hull) - Use this term to express the opinion that an item is too costly.

3. Reduced price?: "Arachu venuma?" (uh-ruh-choo vay-noo-mah) - Say this when attempting to bargain for a lower price.

4. Good quality: "Nalla quality" (nul-lah kwah-luh-tee) - Ask about a product's quality by using this expression.

Language Advice

1. Learn Basic Tamil: Even though English is widely spoken in Chennai, knowing a few basic Tamil words will improve your ability to communicate with locals and traverse the city.

2. Speak Slowly and Clearly: Use a slow, clear voice when speaking English, particularly when interacting with those who might not be native speakers.

3. Use Gestures: If speaking is difficult for you, express yourself visually or with hand gestures.

4. Be Respectful: Regardless of the language barrier, always show respect when talking with natives. Bridging linguistic and cultural divides can be accomplished in large part with a smile and kind manner.

You may travel more successfully in Chennai, interact with people more successfully, and have a better overall trip experience by being familiar with these helpful expressions and linguistic advice.

RECAP

Chennai, the cultural hub of South India, leaves you with recollections of its energetic streets, fascinating past, and friendly people.

From the imposing Mahabalipuram temples to the serene Marina Beach shoreline, Chennai has enthralled your senses and created a lasting impression on your travels.

Enduring Advice for Vacationers

Here are a few last suggestions to make sure your trip to Chennai ends smoothly and with memories before you leave:

Drink plenty of water

The tropical weather in Chennai can be harsh, particularly in the summer. Throughout your visit, make sure to remain hydrated by drinking lots of water.

Welcome to the Chaos

Chennai's lively marketplaces and busy streets may appear chaotic at first, yet they are evidence of the life and energy of the city. Accept the commotion and lose yourself in the sights, sounds, and fragrances of this vibrant city.

Sample the Local Food

With a diverse array of flavours and scents just waiting to be discovered, Chennai is a food lover's dream come true. Don't pass up the chance to try regional specialties at traditional restaurants and food stands, like dosas, idlis, and biryanis.

Honour regional traditions

Since Chennai is a very traditional and culturally rich city, it's important to observe local etiquette and customs. When visiting places of worship, dress modestly, take off your shoes before entering temples, and give the locals a polite "vanakkam" or "namaste."

Goodbye, Chennai

Take a minute to consider the events and memories you have shared as you get ready to leave Chennai and continue your adventure.

Whether you've visited historic temples, enjoyed fiery street cuisine, or partied all night long in vibrant nightclubs, Chennai will always hold a special place in your heart.

Remember that Chennai will always welcome you back with open arms and be eager to share fresh experiences and discoveries as you wish the city farewell.

Chennai's lively atmosphere and kind greetings will make sure that your memories of the city last long after you've said goodbye, whether it's your first or tenth visit.

Thus, "poyittu varugiren Chennai" (I will return to Chennai) until we cross paths again. I hope your journey is full of happiness, excitement, and the essence of Chennai's rich cultural past.

Have a safe journey, and goodbye to Chennai!

Printed in Great Britain
by Amazon